CLANS OF MANY NATIONS

CLANS OF MANY NATIONS

SELECTED POEMS : 1969-1994

PETER BLUE CLOUD
: ARONIAWENRATE :

WHITE PINE PRESS : FREDONIA, N.Y.

Acknowledgements:
Some of these poems previously appeared in:
Turtle, Bear & Wolf (Akwesasne Press, 1976),
Back Then Tomorrow (Blackberry Press, 1978),
White Corn Sister (Strawberry Press, 1979).

I wish to thank the editors of the numerous magazines
and anthologies in which many of these poems have appeared.

Publication of this book was made possible, in part,
by grants from the National Endowment for the Arts
and the New York State Council on the Arts.

Cover print: "Dreamer" ©1994 by Louis Blue Cloud

Book design: Elaine LaMattina

Manufactured in the United States of America.

First printing 1995

10 9 8 7 6 5 4 3 2 1

Published by White Pine Press
10 Village Square
Fredonia, New York 14063

For my children:
Meyo
Louis
Rainy

Contents

CLANS OF MANY NATIONS

Preface

"Blue Cloud's poems are living proof that the power and beauty of the Old Ways cannot be lost." I wrote for Peter Blue Cloud's *Turtle, Bear, and Wolf* when it first came out. This larger collection with much new work confirms that—and more.

The incredibly refined little cultures of subsistence and place—all over the world—that have informed human life for tens of thousands of years, are evaporating away now. Whole languages have been disappearing like summer snowfields, and invaders still come in waves—waves of merchants, tourists, and bureaucrats, as well as armies. Whole forests, herds of elk, bison pronghorn, have left us. And the deep sense of gratitude to the whole natural world that was once a key part of human feelings and manners is rarely heard expressed. Where has that fine grace gone?

Is it all lost? Was it ever real? A life where men and women, trees, grasses, animals, the wind were at ease with each other? Virtually spoke to each other? Now we must be part of the grey modern world: "be realistic," some say, as they lean forward and switch on the television set.

Much of Blue Cloud's work stands squarely in the mode of twentieth century American poetry. But he has lived through territories most poets haven't even dreamed of and explores them with many voices—narrative, lyrical, celebratory, mythic, interspecies. His Native American stance is fresh, personal, and original. And he dedicates his work not to any tribe or group but to "all peoples." He invents nothing; speaks from his own heart and life. The poems echo the contradictions, political madnesses and public disasters that mark the late Twentieth Century, but they leave hope for a renaissance of that intimate life of subsistence with neighbors, gardens, and wildlands that Blue Cloud evokes so splendidly. Such a world will come (to quote one of Peter's titles) "back then tomorrow."

So glimmering from below in these poems, like the moon in the water, is that special eye, that light, which is of the true mind-Nature; human nature one with Mother Nature, which is no particular nature. On this continent, that teaching is still taught in the Old Way.

> the shoots
> give life to eyes
> which see
> > again
> > the people.

Can it come again? It is always here. "Old" means true, right, normal in the flow of the universe. Old also because it is the basic way to live—Taoism, Hinduism, Buddhism are the younger brothers, slightly confused because of passing through the temporary turbulence called civilizaton. "Old" because available to all—regardless of culture, race, or place who will set themselves down to the ground of their minds. We go about our cusp-of-the-century fossil-fuel-fired tasks trying to keep in touch with that vast resonance.

> At winter's table
> > may we all
> think upon
> > the first green shoots
> those gone
> > and those to come.

— Gary Snyder

12

CLANS OF MANY NATIONS

White Corn Sister

first speaker

It was Crow, with beak and belly
full of seed corn
who flew into the face of the sun
    burning,
and through the smokehole of night
blackened,
dropping here and there the sacred
    seed corn
to the people far below.

    And Crow left a cry
    of joyful pain heard
    within the breast,
    and left a dance
    remembered even until
    this very morning;

and reached the sunrise seas
to turn again with an arrow
flight of geese who cried
the skypath clear into echos
of seasons promised.

    And the shadow of Crow
    was a huge raven image
    spread across valleys
    and climbing hills,
    And Crow was offspring
    and brother to Raven;

and when they had dropped
all the seeds to earth below
    they flew
to a land of frozen lakes
and there circled one another
    faster, ever faster
to become a void
a whirlpool mystery
    a final line
between worlds.

second speaker:

And the child was graceful
and her dance was gentle
and her tiny feet danced
the seed corn into earth.

She was without clan or tribe,
    an orphan
found wandering upon naked stone,
and the hunter who found her
carried her to his people.

And the hunter's son loved
    the very sight of her
and gladly helped her
loosen the soil around
the green and tender plants.

And the seasons cared for them,
and the forest called to them
    through the voice of cedar,
and when they slept
the little people of the forest

watched over them and gave
them many dreams.

And like the corn, they grew
to maturity in their season,
then joined hands in promise
to share all the wonders
    of Creation together,
                    forever.

the woman:

I weep still for joy the compassion
of these, my people,
who took me as their own
    without question.

My heart sings through the long
dark of night my silent joy,
my body warmed by his
    and ours in turn
warming these little ones,
    our offspring.

    I was born of a dream
    upon naked stone,
    and the dreamer traced
    the journey of Crow,
    and the living green of corn
    gave me flesh and bones.

And the dream became reality
    when a nation was born,
and it was corn that built a village
and cleared fields to blend the forest.

Now it was that hunters kept
the warming fires of home
within their breasts while traveling;
and winter was a warmer season
within the many lodges.

We emerged from dreaming
to dance a larger dance,
then back into dreams
a few would venture,
        to bring back messages,
of a world before Creation
and the beginnings of man,
of dances and songs
to cure body and mind.

Through the mind of Creation we
were given the sacred ceremonies,
and given to know
that the very universe
is a round dance in time
ever returning to beginnings.

The pebbles and stars, the dust
of earth in hottest summer,
        all elements
possess the life force,
        the mystery,
which is the spirit of the Creation.
Perhaps in my yesterday
I was part of the earthworm
        tunneling and turning
the soils of earth to richness.

I cannot know my tomorrow

but can rejoice
that I am one with earth.

the man:

And for me the hunt is my robe,
be it deer, or elk, or forest path
leading from darkness to light.

I trace the stars at night
camped upon some river's shore,
seeking the pathway of reason.

And often a cold and biting wind
will freeze the earth to whiteness
     and empty snares
     and disturbing dreams
become part of my solitude.

Hungered and blinded, then,
     I must eat
of my own turmoil
and cry aloud the pain
which blinds the mind to reason.

     Then sleep again
will numb my anguish
and in a state of non-dreaming
my spirit finds rest
     and I awaken
to the sunlight of the Creation,
     like a child.

I return to our village
cold and still hungry

to meet other hunters
with the same look
    in their eyes.

I eat a small portion
of what food remains
and chance to meet the eyes
    of my woman,
and there, so deep within her eyes
I see my own anguish reflected,
    and the burden of my shame
is gently lifted from me.

I dream those eyes of hers
and the quiet ways of her motion,
    and the warmth of our children
sleeping so close, enters my dream,
and my dream becomes a chant.

        We are a family
        within a clan within
        a tribe, a nation,
        we are born a nation.

And my dream hears a sound,
    a soft whimper
as a child turns in sleeping
    and I reach
and touch a waiting hand,
and wonder if this strange woman
I know so well and
I do not know at all,
    can also share my dream.

medicine man:

I, too, was given a dream,
    a dream I feared
    and did not want.
I stood trembling within the mystery,
my eyes tightly shut,
my body embraced, and crushed
until I could not breathe.

I swayed and was sick
    wanting desperately
to enter that final sleep.

I was surrounded by good and by evil,
tearing at my muscles and sinews.
    "No!" I cried aloud,
"No! I do not want any of this!"
    Thunder and lightning
    danced my mind,
I was naked and cold,
    I was so afraid.

I entered the dreaming of the hunter,
entered the dark world of his anguish,
    I stood at the center
    of his pain
and was given to recognize
the dark twin of the Creation.

I saw men standing on cliffs
above rock-filled ravines,
    who would cast themselves
    down, down to death.
This, too, is yours, a voice

seemed to say, as I watched
men begin to scream a rage
and foam at mouth and mind
for the remainder of their lives.

We are born twins of good and evil
in one body, and I knew,
oh, yes, I knew long before
the vision was forced upon me.

I realized that I was not in a dream
but standing in a cloud world
between Creation and my own mind.
And from the swirling mists
on my right appeared a sacred rattle,
and from the swirling mists
on my left there floated to me
the wings of an eagle,
        and I took each.

And I saw directly before me
a small plant in flower,
a green and gentle-seeming plant,
        and I knew
the leaves of that plant,
and had lived in its roots,
and knew its essence,
        its power
                to cure.

And living many lifetimes
with the plant, I was given
to know many others, each
carrying me to the next,

and the first song I was given
was a personal law and warning,
     to cure
and only to cure
     and never, ever
to use these powers for gain.

     This nation
each and every one of us,
     we are a voice,
                    a song,
no person more or less than another
     all is sacred, we are sacred,
for we are children
of the Creation.
     And the song
we are given must always
echo into tomorrow.
     And the drum
we have fashioned is the heartbeat
of all things living.
     And the rattle
is the wind and storm
and the tall, dry corn,
                    dancing.
clan mother:

And the tall, dry corn
is picked and braided
and hung within the lodge.

We give thanks to the Creation
that our children will be fed,
we offer a prayer to all
things within the Creation.

The waterdrum and rattle,
the deep voiced singer,
the circle of people in dance
    is our praise,
our hearts pumping blood
    is our promise.

    I am old, I sit wrapped
    warmly, close to the fire,
        my eyes, though dimmed
    see clearly the dancers.

I touch the fabric of my childhood
and remember,
          the hunger,
and remember a people scattered,
    in mind and body.

The Creation took pity upon us
and gave us White Corn Sister,
and through the power of this gift
    we were born a nation.

And season merged into season
    and we learned
the life cycles of all
    around us,
like the moon, the face of each
thing is in constant change
    and yet
life goes into death a seed
    awaiting rebirth.

And season into season
we grew into a nation

of many lodges
    and cornfields,
and ceremonies were given us
as were beans and squash.

And we sat in council
    male and female
to ponder the future of our children,
    of our nation,
and again Creation heard
and answered with the voices
    of our elders.

And season into season
like the sapling pine
grew the thinking of our elders
into a great tree,
and the laws by which
our nation was to live
became known as the Great Good.
And these laws were like
    seeds of corn,
each separate, yet bound
    to a single core,
and these laws were spoken
often to our people
    that none forget.

And the memory of these laws
were woven into beaded belts
    like rows of seed corn,
and the words were said
to the hearts and minds
    of the people
as a living part of life

and not mere words
to drift away upon a breeze.

I am old, I dream smiling,
sitting in the sun, the children
pass and greet me: "Grandmother,
it is a beautiful day."
And truly, it is.

first speaker:

And season followed season
as our nation grew,
the child became grandparent
    became ancestor,
the nation thrived with
the gift of corn.

There was pain and hunger
in their seasons,
a reminder to the people
that life, though strong
is but a thread in the Creation.

second speaker:

And the twin of evil ways
often overshadowed the good,
and greed and envy were known,
    but always
the Great Good was remembered
and the strength of clan mothers
spoke through the chiefs
and brought reason
    to the people.

the woman:

And again there was peace
for many, many seasons.
Then a child was born
whose dreaming disturbed the nation.

He was given visions of destruction
and bloodshed never before known.
    And these things,
these horrors,
            came to be.

the hunter:

The child grew to manhood
only to die,
            himself childless,
but brother to a nation.
He lay bleeding upon
a burned and blackened cornfield,
the smoldering remains
of a village close by.

He smiled at the thought of death
    and waited
until others of his people
could hear his whispered words:
    that a nation was born
    of a Great Good,
and that a nation thus born
must remain strong
    even to the death
    of its people:

"The twins of good and evil
have merged into a creature
    of two minds,
giving with one hand
and destroying with the other.
It is begun, for I have seen it,
    the great destruction.

"Already our nation is scattered,
our villages and cornfields lie
wasted and dying, and this
    is but the beginning,
for I have visioned the destruction
lasting many lifetimes.

"Lasting so long that the children
of tomorrow will accept
and even live within the evil.
"I have seen the nations
of this earth scattered and destroyed,
wandering in hungered groups
devouring the very seeds
which lie sleeping, awaiting
    their season.

"A plague of greed will tear
and destroy the very earth,
and the very air and waters
will fill with man's foulness,
and his gift to earth and Creation
will be his own hidden desire:
    to perish once and for all
and forever, to have done
with the Creation.

"Horrible was the vision to behold,
    and yet
hovering over it, and enfolding it
at all times
was the hand of the twin of good.

"And the mind of the good spoke to me
and left a promise.
A promise of life in the midst
of death, if we but
kept the Great Good alive
within our nation.

"We were to be a nation scattered,
    a people lost.
In our loneliness we were to seek
one another, to counsel again
and be of one mind,
living in the midst of death
we were to live the Great Good,
    live it in truth,
and not as the mouthing of words.

"The seed corn in earth,
the newborn child,
the sun rising as ever
to warm the good earth,
    all these
in promise to a scattered nation."

medicine man:

So was it spoken and remembered
by a scattered people,
remnants of a nation.

So did they seek
to keep the fires
of the Great Good alive.

And even into today,
in the heart of this nation,
the Great Good lives,
held by a few threads of sinew
which must be gathered
into a strong and binding cord.

This sinew, these threads of life
connecting elder to child
and child to Creation,
is the meaning of our mystery.

We, the elders, are gatherers
of this thread,
we are the singers who send
our voices to the directions
calling our children
to return, to be reborn a nation.

Come home to us and touch
    our hands,
and lift the soil and smell
the rich, damp earth,
yours forever in promise.

Return to us and dance
the praise of the Great Good
and sit with us in council
close to the warming hearth.

clan mother:

And season follows season
and born a nation
we plant the sacred corn,

and do you see your elder
back bent with age
hoe in hand
slowly walking to the cornfield?

And will you bend beside him
and hear his whispered words,
that he welcomes home his children,
    and that now,
when his eyes close
upon that final sleep
his journey will be in peace?

    I am old, and these bones
    of mine protest each move,
        but the sun is warm, my children.

Will you listen further,
will you hear the words
of this old woman,
    this clan mother?

Counsel wisely with your elders
then counsel your mind and heart
and do not trust yourself to speak
of the Great Good
    until your mind and heart are one.

Offer advice only if you have tasted

of the turmoil in question,
and be strong inside and truly believe
before using the outward power
of your voice to convince
others of your truth.

And when a feast is given,
thank the Creation that
the people have food to eat.

And eat the corn and squash and beans
knowing that your back has bent
to the rhythm of the hoe.

And at the fire's warming glow
be pleased that you have shared
in the gathering of the fuel
to keep warm the lodge.

And know and praise the seasons
in the knowledge that you
have shared their constant change.

And let yourself change
as do the seasons, and grow
in mind, spirit and body
for your nation, your people.

    I sigh; do you hear?
    The sun is setting
    and evening's first cool breeze
    is felt by my old body.

I will enter the lodge now.
Grandaughter, is there corn

within reach that I
may shell for evening's meal?

Grandson, I see that you
have piled the wood
close at hand
to warm the night's cold.

If I call to you in the night,
comfort an old woman
with your answer.
I look at these old, wrinkled hands
which have done so much,
    my eyes blur,
I tremble with age,
I find myself whispering
to my own departed parents.

    Grandchildren, sit
    by this old woman
    that she may know
        that a nation lives.

First Brother

I bind the sinew tight
      arrow to foreshaft
feather to base
      power to arm
swift deer, I dream your eyes
brother so fast, I drift upon a wing
our grandfather has touched us both
who fashions the mountain's climb

to approach that sacred spring
      to sweat the body to sky
brother deer, you stand in wonder
      and my heart and finger bleed

I pull the bow tight
      arrow to sinew
my brother, I sing you forever
      strength for my child

For A Child

Circle the mountain gently
        for the mountain is gentle
think of the open valley
        on the other side
think through the mountain
        of the open valley on the other side
there may be danger there
        or hurt in that open place

think in a circle
        around this gentle mountain
and soon the mountain
        will become as crystal
and you will see the open valley
        through the crystal mountain
and all the truth of the mountain
        and valley will be yours

and circle the mountain gently
        and gently enter
        that peaceful valley
where the crystal's heart
        has its lodge.

Death Chant

buffalo, buffalo, buffalo, buffalo
   running
   thundering
   stampede
quenching life

slaughtered
   we die the buffalo
slaughtered
   we die
       the buffalo
slaughtered
   the buffalo we die
butchered
   my song continues
grizzly, grizzly, grizzly, grizzly
   o, bear
       o, turtle
         I sing.

Little Fawn

Girl Child so quiet and watchful
    all songs are sung for you alone,
who are your mother's pride,
    a father's quest in strength,
who enters tomorrow stepping lightly
    upon a multitude of willing hearts,

    all songs your blanket,
    all tribes your people,
    little girl child,
    sing us many rainbows.

Glacier Country

white cloud
wind-worn
feather etchings,

golden eagle
soaring
air
piercing crystal
cry,

snow fields
sun breath
cascading,

torrents white
foam misting
mountain voices,

feathered shaft
moon dawn
naked stone,

owl stories
echoing hollow
dry burnt
blackened snag,

sounding board
woodpecker tapping
chipmunks join
day's round dance.

Alcatraz

As lightning strikes the Golden Gate
and fire dances the city's streets,
a Navajo child whimpers the tide's pull
and Sioux and Cheyenne dance lowly the ground.

Tomorrow is breathing my shadow's heart
and a tribe is an island, and a tribe is an island,
and silhouettes are the Katchina dancers
of my beautiful people.

Heart and heaven and spirit
written in a drum's life cycle
and a tribe is an island, forever,
forever we have been an island.

As we sleep our dreaming in eagles,
a tribe is an island
and a tribe is a people
in the eternity of Coyote's mountain.

When's the Last Boat to Alcatraz?

(for Richard Oakes)

When's the last boat to Alcatraz?
    I hear the foghorns and lonely gulls.
Who's skipper on that leaky tub,
    the Broken Treaty,
and what people drum and chant
    upon that turtle now?

It grows darker here, within this forest.
    They try to tell me that my brother died.
I laugh and my laughter echoes,
    through these redwoods
    breaking inner light.
I laugh and laugh and hear a pistol shot,
which is a loose rock falling from
    the cliff on Alcatraz.

A lone bear walks the wooded mountains
    of Pomo country, of Pit River country.
A tall bear, whose anger is a sometimes
    earthquake
    of gentle thunder.

When's the last treaty being written?

It is ten seconds to America, 1976.

It grows darker still as the sky eagle
folds those great wings
    upon my brother's sleep.
It is winter and the glaciers descend
    upon the cities,

the harbors freeze over and the tug
boat "Good Citizen" is trapped
        between Alcatraz and myth.
It is cold and even the temperature
        of memory
        slows its course.

The breath of that lone bear
        is snuffing loudly
        among the giant redwoods.

When's the last boat to Alcatraz?
        (It was so cold and damp,
so little food,
        the children's laughter.
That fog we remember, out there.
        We played shadow games.
Close to fire's heat the drum's taut need,
        and our need
                a warmth of dancing.)

Such strange visions upon that rock.
        Hey, yes,
                these are tears
                        at last.

Told never to say that name again, and
told to dream of other islands,
        dreaming instead
                of a bear,
                not lonely, but,
dancing slowly and heavily.

My brother, Stands Tall, his name,
        now we wish his journey
                be in peace.

Composition

there was the buffalo blowing
blood and steam from throat wound
and even the smell of gore and
of fear mingling hate anger,
the sound of the great heart
                    thumping,
   and a leg convulsively pawing
a furrow, and already
               the first flies,
the hunter's desperate pull upon
   the short thrusting spear, ashamed
of his poor aim causing
   such pain to his brother,
   desperately
wanting to plunge again,
              true
to end mutual pain,
and the horse standing trembling
and frothing from the wild
   ecstacy of the chase,
   and a plain,
and mountains and glorious clouds,

all such a rich canvas,
and beyond the easel, a bare
               white wall
and the inner image of a composition
   beyond manipulation.

untitled

Walking thru twisted hollow pathways
hand in hand under blue
sky tracings of wispy question
marks the flight of gulls
and this land is green and this land
trembles with old and young
lovers loose-footing adventure
into golden autumns and winter
cabins the wood smoke sharp

bite of axe to tree to ground
the sting of sweat a pungent odor
of climbing hills the deer's delicate
steps to stars the universe of grasses
bared to swaying breezes the likes
of elderberry flutes melodious
quivering fingers of sound the lap
and shush of gentle waves on sand
the lake a turquoise feast platter
overflowing with an abundance

of many flavored delicacies
savored the tang of rootlets
plucked from mud the pond
awaiting the evening loon's
practiced mirror laughter
the chuckling canoe cutting
waters the river directs to sea
and harbors close the salmon
spawn a million tiny eyes
direct the passage of the sun
to mountains unseen mystery
stories recited upon a feathered down

flight the eagle stone thrown
to ground the twang of bowstring
vibration of wings the hummingbird
slapped tail shout of echoes the beaver

sniffs the otter's nose cruising by
willows their roots entangling
dream flights their arrow leaves
spear sunlight in shadow flecks
dappled the frog coat and croak
bristling fur the wolverine dances
sideways and round fallen antlers
of oak trees and sugarpine first frost
the valleys crack and split back
and forth the saws of crickets
night song again the bullfrog
bass bellow the lilypad chewings
snout glistening moose twitching
ears the child buffalo bawling
tentative tangle of unsteady legs

stiffenend now the hunter's poise
upon tears blurring aim and deed
and deed the earth to brother wolf
teeth grinding corn the grandmother
sings rabbit songs the grandchild
forgetting owl's warnings hooted
the cradle song of night worlds
without end the star dance across
sky path the night hawk's sacred
shadows within shadows deep
furry chirping chitters the fallen tree

of moss and memories hanging
tangled hair the ancient cedar

raven roost and wonderment
the dawn's first dove cooing
rocks the gentle cradle breeze
faint embers the fire's warmth
breathes the new day glorious
orange, red, purple, blue
and giggles the child awakened
into day.

Tomorrow

We have wept the bloods of countless ages
    as each of us raised high the lance of hate,
ours is the beauty of foreverness, if we but
    accept that which our Creator freely gives.
Now let us dry our tears and learn the dance
    and chant of the life cycle.
Tomorrow dances behind the sun in sacred promise
    of things to come for children not yet born,
for ours is the potential of truly lasting beauty
    born of hope and shaped by deed.
Now let us lay the lance of hate upon this oil
    that hands may join in dance our mother earth,
and lodges build with eastern-facing doors
    that always the sun may witness a praise
of family and kin and creatures and creation
    knowing a harmony of guardianship
each to each, and far into tomorrow.
    Now we have spoken, who are your brothers.

Turtle

The winds are dark passages among the stars,
leading to whirling void pockets
encircled by seeds of thought,
life force of the Creation;
    I am turtle,
and slowly, my great flippers move
propelling my body through space,
and starflowers scatter crystals
which fall as mist upon my lidded eyes.
    I am turtle,
and the ocean of my life swim
is a single chant in the Creation,
as I pass others my kind,
    my own, unborn, and those,
the holy ancients of my childhood.

My swim is steady and untiring
for great is the burden given me,
the praise and privilege of my eternity
rests upon my back as a single seed
to which I am guardian and giver.
    I am turtle,
and my tribes forever remain countless,
from the day I first raised my head
to gaze back upon the horn of my body,
    and my head was a sun,
    and Creation breathed life upon the seed
    and four times, and again four times,
    I wept for joy the birthing of my tribes,
    and chanted Creation the glory
of all these wonderous days.

The wrinkles and cracks upon this ancient shell

are the natural contours created
by the feel and request of burdened rock
and soil, blood and sustenance to
clans within clans,
      I am turtle,
and the earth I carry is but
a particle in the greater Creation,
my mountains, plains and oceans,
mere reflections in a vaster sea.
        Turtle, I am called,
        and breathe clouds of rain,
        and turn slowly my body to seasons
        in cycle with my grandchild, Eagle,
        whose wings enfold thunder pulses,
        back to back, and
seldom meeting in time.

Patience was given me by Creation,
ancient song on tomorrow's wind,
this chant that was taught my tribes
is now unsung by many clans
of a single tribe,
      and truly
such pains that exist for this moment,
which slay so many of the innocent
cannot but end in pain repeated
as all are reflected twins to self.
      I am turtle,
and await the council of my tribes
clan into clan, the merging thought
that evil was never the star path, and
then the chant to the four directions,
      I am turtle,
and death is not yet my robe,
for drums still throb the many

centers of my tribes, and a young
child smiles me of tomorrow,
    "and grandparent,"
another child whispers, "please,
tell again my clan's beginning."

A Hunt, Its Chant

now when we depart
upon this newest hunt
let it be grandfather,
    song of our people.

now from the village
our old ones chant,
great is our honor,
    we see their hunger.

now when we camp
we seek ancient strength,
our dreams call deer,
    in pity call deer.

now to the Creator
our minds open out,
we are but children,
    hear us, our prayer.

grandfather,
    grandfather,
this is all.

grandfather,
    grandfather,
a hungry people.

Camp

by starlight hush of wind the owl's shadow voice,
the campfire embers glowing inner universe,
by firelight smoke curls weaving faint the voices,
coyote voices faint the pain & smell of pitch,
  fire, I sing you stars,
  fire, I breathe obsidian
& again the owl's shadow voice leans back
into times past
  singing first fire,

brittle spine bent bowed toward the fire,
voices low to murmur a child whimper,
deer fat sucked upon to gentle dreaming
the mother her song the night cradles,
  child, the owl, too, has young,
  tiny hearts & warmth of down,
& old man coughing gutteral spit to fire,
young people giggle beneath hide-fondlings
  soon to sleep,

again coyote voices crowd the mind in a loneliness
of deep respect in love of those who camp
  just up the hill,
& tiny crystals of tears spatter the dust,
  my people,
legs that cannot ever carry me back to you,
  soul that holds you
  forever.

Dawn

in balance, the moon & dawn cast equal light & shadows
        are twins of a single core
the pines of black their webs of branches lean toward the dawn
        in that first touch of wind,
        that ancestor murmur, gentle sweep across earth,
as stars & crickets begin their harmony of sleep, one by one
        gone into silence,
& momentarily, a vast quiet settles all, then a snapping twig
        betrays a tentative step,
& again the quiet, but for the echo of coyote cries heard earlier.

the campfire speaks a low, soft crackling & smoke is the story
        of surrounding growth,
odor of smoked deermeat tempts the mind like tiny, sharpened
        hooves,
& coffee is early morning wine fermented in the glowing coals
        of welcome heat.

a first bold chirping in a sapling oak, a startled answer
        from the pinenut tree,
& suddenly there never was a silence, as blue jay tells on
        flicker, "he did it! he did it!"
& dawn is bright reality in newborn day,
& will the hawk, cry soon.

Bear - A Totem Dance As Seen by Raven

(for Ranoies)

The black bear does a strange and shuffling dance
foot to foot slowly, head back, eyes closed
    like that of a man.
Beneath a loosely falling robe,
mouth sewn shut upon protruding tongue
    of red-stained cedar shreddings.
Foot to foot slowly in lumbering
                shadow dance
within the fog and rain of high, thick ferns,
beneath a dripping, tapping spruce,
    echo of raven
morning cry of night visions unwanted.

A heavy, leaning snag it seems at first
the sound of crashing fall
        suspended
    between ground and lowered sky.
then swirl of fog unveils
        a huge head
carved atop the pole, a silver-grey of cedar.

Gnashing of angry teeth at driftwood shore
and killer whale spews up
        a wreckage
    of pock-infested sailors.

Foot to foot slowly, the totem dance continues,
sky to earth the leaning weight
        of pole
    and people and bear
    and now the drum,

53

rectangular and fringed with clacking claws.

A chant begins of deep-voiced rumbling,
of the black slate carved
                    into bowls now broken
with fragments scattered in despair
              of a death not prophesied.

Great cedar poles in moist earth,
these dwellings speak with dark passages,
          (the rib of a tribe is a brittle section
                              of a dugout
        or what is left
                    of a stolen house post,
              vast heritage dragged
                    into strange museums)

and still, and forever, foot to foot slowly
the strange and shuffling dance continues.
And day after day the mourning chants
and keening voices silence all else
                    as dugouts
          with quiet paddles
convey the dead to sacred islands
          in endless procession.

And soil seeps through roof cracks to fill
the huge and silent dwellings.
And totems lean from which
                    great eyes
gaze either up to sky or down to earth,
and the death of a village is a great sorrow,
and the pain of the survivors
          is a great anguish
                    never to heal.

Slowly and gently
                    foot to foot balanced
and awkward in beauty
                    the child dances.
And grandfather taps,
                    delicately taps
the drum and his voice is very, very low,
          and the song is a promise
          given a people
in the ancient days of tomorrow.

And grandmother's stiff
                    and swollen fingers
weave cedar and fern and spruce,
          and occasionally
          in a far away closeness
her eyes seek the dancing child.

The bear pauses in his quest for food
          to stand and sniff the air
then in a dream like a fasting
                    he begins
          to shuffle
          foot to foot slowly
as the dance continues.

Crazy Horse Monument

Hailstones falling like sharp blue sky chips
howling winds the brown grass bends, while
buffalo paw and stamp and blow billowing steam,
and prairie wolves chorus the moon in moaning.

The spotted snake of a village on the move
a silent file of horses rounding hills,
in a robe of grey, the sky chief clutches thunder
and winter seeks to find the strongest men.

      Crazy Horse rides the circle of his people's sleep,
             from Little Big Horn to Wounded Knee,
      Black Hills, their shadows are his only robe
             dark breast feathers of a future storm.

Those of broken bodies piled in death,
of frozen blood upon the white of snow,
yours is now the sky chant of spirit making,
pacing the rhythm of Crazy Horse's mount.

And he would cry in anger of a single death,
and dare the guns of mounted soldiers blue,
for his was the blood and pulse of rivers,
and mountains and plains taken in sacred trust.

      Crazy Horse rides the circle of his people's sleep,
             from Little Big Horn to Wounded Knee,
      Black Hills, their shadows are his only robe
             dark breast feathers of a future storm.

And what would he think of the cold steel chisel,
and of dynamite blasting mountain's face,
what value the crumbled glories of Greece and Rome,

to a people made cold and hungry?

To capture in stone the essence of a man's spirit,
to portray the love and respect of children and elders,
fashion instead the point of a hunting arrow sharp,
and leave to the elements the wearing-down of time.

Crazy Horse rides the circle of his people's sleep,
from Little Big Horn to Wounded Knee,
Black Hills, their shadows are his only robe
dark breast feathers of a future storm.

To-ta Ti-om

(for an aunt)

my aunt was an herb doctor, one-eyed with crooked yellow teeth
    the Christians called her pagan witch
    and their children taunted her
    or ran in fear of their bible lives
        at her approach,
her house of barn lumber leaned into the wind as if toppling
    in winter it grew squat with snow
    and bright sparks from the wood stove
    hissed the snowflakes into steam
        icing the roof,
"when my body dies it will be in winter just in time for spring"
    she told this while rolling leaves
    to powder between her bony hands
    for her duty as a medicine person
        was to cure,
in early summer grandfather and I would begin planting
    the corn and beans and squash
    just behind my aunt's house
    and she'd hobble over to help
        plant the tobacco,
as the first green shoots emerged into sunlight
    she would sit on the steps
    grating dried roots into a bowl
    stopping every so often to gaze
        at the garden,
when the time of tobacco curing came she'd be there
    feeling and smelling and tasting
    and every season she would approve
    then later sit by the woodstove
        smoking her pipe,
"Come," she would say to me, "the time for onanoron is here,"
    and we would walk to the pond

and she would point out strong plants
for me to wade to and slowly pull
those medicine roots,
we strung the roots of twisted brown above the woodstove
to preserve their sacred power
to be released as needed
by those who had need
of such strength,
tiny bundles were made of the roots with bits of string
then she named the persons
I was to take onanoron to
and tied all in a blue bandana
and said, "Go,"
this is for Kaienwaktatse and this for Kaerine, and
Lives-Close-to-Town
and She-Bends-the-Boughs
a penny or two and bread and jam
I shyly ate,
the pennies slowly filled the glass jar on the table
until my aunt went to the store
a block of salt pork one finger square
a nutmeg, salt and four candies
just for me,
sitting there by the woodstove I would steal a glance
at her tired wrinkled face
and I'd want to shout loud
feeling a tightening in my throat
and maybe cry,
"she was sitting at her table with a bowl in her lap
and it was just turning Spring,"
my grandfather wrote this to me
and I went somewhere to be alone
and just sat,
it's planting time again and all done except tobacco
grandfather's leaning on the hoe

and looking at my aunt's house
then he smiles and I smile back
lonely, like crying.

Wolf

burrowing deep into earth until the grave is complete
hiding in daytime shadows, panting,

                        sweat,
        dry matted blood
        and stump of a leg,
wolf, his growls into whimpers of pain unending.

she-wolf keening the stiffened, frozen cubs,
licking the frosted muzzles cyanide tracings, sweet
            the steaming meat
            she gently places
as an offering, though she knows they are dead.

run down to earth and snow with bursting heart
down to the bright red hammering pulse, and further
                                down
            one by one
            the rifle shot
echo resounding a terrible, alien blood lust.

protruding, blackened tongues, no more the night chant,
blanket of sound, the earth her moaning,
                         futile,
            her emptied womb,
            and the seed
dried and rustling among forgotten leaves.

a wind of running leaves across the prairie,
a scent of pine in frozen north the muskeg
            lakes
                lent footprints
            cast in sandstone
grains rubbing time the desert's constant edge.

softly contoured voices moaning night,
the wolves in circle council the moon
                    shadows
                              bent starlight
                    of fingered sleet
rattles the gourd of earth down feathered roots.

beyond beginnings the earth her many tribes
and clans their life songs merge into one
                    chant
                              welcome dance
                    to the unborn
awaiting birth in the sun-fingered dawn.

and to each creation the heartline trail
is etched in delicate memory pattern
                    webs
                              so intricate
                    in a unity
of day into night the seasons follow.

the moaning low of wolves to ears of men
first wisdom gained by another's quiet
                    song
                              of meditation
                    circle of council
bound together by their basic power.

and the quiet way of learning was the food
and spark the hearth of compassion warm
                    enfolding
                              all others
                    born of earth
in the harmony of mutual need.

in thanks the minds of curious men
sought further wisdom from the brother
                wolf
                    his clan
                a social order
of strength through lasting kinship,

and recognized the she-wolf's place
in balance with that of the male leader
                heads
                    of family
                to be obeyed
because their first law was survival,

and studied the pattern of the hunt
where each had a particular role
                defined
                    by need
                and acted upon
without the slightest hesitation,

and moaning low the wolf song,
head bent the drummer and voice to sky
                singer
                    in thanks
                to brother wolf,
now your song will sing in our voices.

again the rifle shot and snapping jaws
of steel traps and poisoned bait,
the bounty hunter and fur trapper
                predators
                    of greed
whose minds create vast lies.

and moaning low in death chant
the one remaining wolf staggers
        and falls
        to death
as winds carry his voice into tomorrow.

and the voice is an accusation howling
within the brain heart pulling sinews
        harshly
        you, too
I hang my death about your neck in circle.

mourn the buffalo and the beaver,
keen the fox and mountain cat,
        shout
        the grizzly
antelope elk moose caribou and many

more gone into death the prime breeders
to fashion garments of vanity,
        Indian,
        brother,
cleanse the blood lust from your naked spirit

and fast and pray your spirit's new growth
and be reborn into childhood innocence
        purity
        our maker
awaits your ancient promise.

the wolf in dream has petitioned
for his voice to be heard in council
        now
        in this place
        let us open our minds.

scattered and lost the people fall,
orphaned, the child feels hunger,
           where is tomorrow,
           where does it hide?

there are four voices coming
from four directions
           the center is harmony
           the center is beginning
scouts and messengers called back,
the council is the mind
           it is merging thought
           the nation's birth.
now when warriors feast,
they eat of embers
           the fire's heat
           stored energy.
the warrior society
is the wolf society
           is the clan family
           heart of tribe.
anger seeking wisdom,
council after meditation
           there is a vision
           held in sacred trust.

I dance upon my three remaining legs,
           look,
the memory of the fourth keeps my balance,
             see,
my wispy white and cyanide fog-breath,
           hah!
taut sinews vibrate the sky's held thunder,
            huh!
steel traps I weave a necklace of your making,
           hah!

puffs of dust I quick-stomp with paw feet,

                         huh!
I am becoming you dancing for them,

                    hah!
I jump upon your back a heavy robe,

                    huh!
my shadow will nip your pumping ankle,

                         huh!
you will think you me in the full moon night,

                              huh!
I crush your long bones sucking marrow,
nose your severed head before me the trail,
tear strips of flesh the ribbons weave a net,
chew hair and fingernails into mash
I slap upon my festered stump your human glue,

                              hah!
now you are dancing,

          brother

                    now you are dancing.

Descent

down gently
through the smokehole down
sky to water gourd
                     down
into shadows down
                     as a child
is being born
                and close
                          by fire
an elder is huddled
awaiting the calm journey
                          down
and sparks
            are star patterns
of dew upon webs
which descend
                and hang
to drop
          upon
              a drum's taut surface.

Yellowjacket

He rode into town upon a wild-eyed mountain horse
his hat pulled low and down his back and shoulders
swaying and blowing in wind, long black and grey hair,
and no one saw the eyes, but even the soldiers felt
themselves being studied, maybe as coldly as the wind blowing
downriver,
man and horse, passing through town in silent watching
stirring along small puffs of dust and leaving behind
the strong odors of buckskin and cedar smoke,
"He carries a pistol besides that rifle," someone said,
and a young and respectful voice said, "a real bad one, too,
        I hear."
an old man, a healer who still dared perform the rituals
of curing, but in hiding from the eyes of soldier and missionary
hummed and muttered an old mountain song under his breath
and whispered, "A spirit rides with him, and he carries
a whole tribe: he is what remains of a tribe, and we, the ghosts."
"Yes," said the sergeant, "another goddamn fence has been
ripped down and dragged until tangled and useless. We give
the heathens a whole valley to live in, but it ain't good
enough for them, should round them up and shoot the lot,
like we was doing before; or at least the real bad ones, especially
        Yellowjacket."
with a half a butchered steer tied to his horse
he approached his sister's tiny shack at the edge of town,
"The deer are moved to the high mountains like me, don't like
the smell of oiled leather and iron stoves. Here is meat
of a kind best left for the buzzards, but meat at least to eat."
Another fence was torn down and three head of cattle
slaughtered, and the meat left at the edge of town, as a dare
to the hungry to take, and to eat and to live a while longer,
and a soldier, too, found with slit throat, a quick and
clean kill and no signs of cruelty or anger, a hunter killed by

the hunted.
and mounted, the soldiers rode through town
and the people watched and knew a longing,
a feeling for a something lost, just out of reach,
but not a one of them mounted a horse or reached for a rifle,
but merely watched and waited, ashamed to raise their eyes to
    one another.
and they saw him, hatless and riding slowly, so slowly
into town, and the clean upriver mountain air wildly
blew his hair about, and as he passed he stared into
the eyes of each with no reproach, and each of them saw
the holes and streaming blood as he rode through their midst
and was never seen again, and the talking, too, stopped
when his sister said to a crowd of them, "Don't speak
of him again, you don't deserve his name," and they
watched her saddle up and take her child
and turn her back upon her husband and home and never
    look back.
and on that same evening, a few youngsters, too, saddled
up and for the first time in many seasons, openly
showed their rifles, and some old people joined them
and they rode upriver, up toward the clean air and
naked stone, and the soldiers saw them pass, and dared
    not interfere.

Shady Creek

eyes searching thru hills of gravel
seeing through to the other side
                                                        stars,
carrying a burden basket of wind
and red-ochred forehead pressed
by a burden strap of night sounds,
swift feet wrapped in oak leaves
and a walking stick of barking
                                                        coyotes,
breathing sharp deer prints
            thinking moisture
split thoughts of fire
forked lightning
                        lips
pressed to sapling bent
as six snow-browed geese
praise sky.

Milkweed

your blood mixed with air
holds the world together,
with your fiber sinews
the bowstring hums
to slightest wind,
your grey-green leaves
are signals of a friendly camp,
and then your seedlings
float gently
like first flakes of snow,
and your empty pods are fashioned
into rattles,
or taken by children
to become canoes
with pebbles for passengers
taken to far-away lands,
and now your yellowed leaves
rustle the music
of another snow
and your seedlings
lie sleeping.

Girl Child

your mother combs your hair
and stars fall at your feet,
hair like the cool night river
dark blue with droplets of moon,
fat little fingers dance and curl
their very own playful stories
    and grandmother's eyes are filled,
and when you sit alone to play
humming your baby song
to wildflowers and tiny bugs
    there is a far away playing
of an elderberry flute
    brought by the wind.

We sit balanced

between
end and beginning
upon the back
    of turtle
and the pools
        of light
    we see in water
is sky deepness roots
        moist earth womb
seedling hawk
            born
screaming joy

    life precious
praise earth
    sky
    water
    sunfire
life spark praise
            forever,
and once
and only once
        until
each is absorbed
through reflected waters
        backward
        into tomorrow
sideways
        sometimes
our dance
        yes,
(ah,
    to dance

                    lightly as
finger weavings
lightly

    as breast down
    floating)
and it is corn
            placed in earth
            a short while
                        ago
and now
        the shoots
give life to eyes
which see
            again
        the people.

Sweat Lodge - The Afterwards

Water on rocks the hiss of steam,
      of sage
dropped rocks into holes in space
the hissing of star-flung meteors,
      No!
yes, it is thought sparks my mind
      is thinking
            maybe
but through all time there is a voice
      singing
shoulder to shoulder squatting among
      mountains
great boulders move and touch
and the sound is a hollowness
      space echo

this lodge is the earth womb
      is the mother time
is the past into future time,

the unborn of our people
      touch my hanging hair,
I shiver, feel a choking
      my chest aches
      as I gulp down steam
      breathe through nose a pure darkness

I am snake stream winding downhill
      belly-slithering among trees
lying in moss I watch companions
      float
above and beyond minds' beginnings
I touch cedar and sage, my nose

tasting,
in a sometime, a pipe,
                    sacred,
then raspberries
and more water
                a singing
            has entered my mind,
a creature circle of chewing
eating away my brain blanket
to open bare my mind to darkness
            as the lodge rocks
back and forth and now spinning
again through space spinning
            the singing,
shoulder nudged again
                        by fur
to sway the other way
                    to touch
        yielding shell
it is they
        then, I am
sitting here between bear
        and turtle
                yes,
        bear and turtle

I reach to feel my chest
        my legs,
                reaching
        with hands and arms
        I do not have,
                    nothing,
I am nothing, no body
        nothing,
        I am a thought

                a seed in space
a blown and scattered thing
                among stars
                            one of many
one of multitudes, circling,
                silent,
then striking the husk
of a larger seed
which also whirls and
                clatters
within yet another

I am nothing, I am all
                I am a part of
                I am a part of
a circle within this lodge
                a cycle
                            in the Mystery!
I hear this and my body jumps
though it is only my neighbor,
                                        coughing,
"Grandfather!"
                        this voice
is from within and without
                it is a shout
                an outcry
but it tapers like a flame
                to a pleading,
                            "Grandfather?"

Then all is fading
                is going
                my selfness
                            fading slowly
through self and into beyond self

        wandering among spirits
among seeds which are thought,
        are pure feeling,

        then a chanting, a song
        and far bck
        from a cavern back

(whisper)
        "Grandfather,
                        I am home."

Sweet Corn

the edge of autumn touches leaves
    and sharpens
    the morning air
white breath the river speaks
in tumbling, slowly tumbling
                        rising
    mists of steam
a biting axe
        is a dog bark
a cracking rifle
        antlers
hollow ringing woods

a crow graws us welcome
    (imagined)
as we harvest sweet corn
the field her summer warmth
    still holds
    in deep, rich earth
                we bend to,
as a running breeze begins
the shushing corn dance
    of our tall sisters
and the sweet grace of their motion
    is the sacred ritual
    of our people.

now, kneeling here upon a blanket
as rain taps lightly the windows,
braiding the sister corn into circlets
to be dried for the season of cold,

    at winter's table

may we all
think upon
      the first green shoots
     those gone
           and those to come.

Autumn Morning

Full moon and the whispering leaves
of dry corn stalks touched by wind
a low mist swirls the river's surface
in gentle dance, like visions lent
by starlight the owl's eyes reflect,
and moon path on water is a walking
murmur of soft questions
   only a child will ask.
and maple's shadow is a pattern
woven by the Creation in balance
of earth and sky,
     then softly
again the owl's call, an inner
sound of warm feathers,
then sudden gust of wind
announces day with a shower
of falling leaves which dance
a frantic, short-lived race.

and dawn is a praise of silence
  to be respected.

She
sings
us
sweetly,
touches
our
feet
with
dance
hands
us
golden
fruit,
hums
us
night
songs
we

ever
taste.

Ochre Iron

Falling forever
with over and under
falling forever from
pink to purple bridgeways
my father's floating, falling,
decays many schemes
in youth's web-footed anger
    of balance.

I wonder how many, if any,
boyhoods my father portrayed
upon my reservation's
    starving soil,
or how many puppies yapped his heels
as over and over he fell,
or which of the mothers
cast shy eyes at fleeing feet,
    and was it this
same lonesome loon
keening his sunset fears.

Falling forever
among wheeling stars
transfixed upon a canvas
    of universes,
my boot's sad dust
in vain retracing
a highway's straight
and naked hostility,
as over and under
    falling forever
I scream
        falling,

as cities collapse to my cry
And layer upon layer of lies
of twisted iron beams and braces
cut limbs searing pains.

I wonder forever how many
if any, stole of rest within
the rich hayloft world
of another's dreaming,
and how many now deserted
campfires cast a warmth
in a taste of winter
found in hidden springs
    along that lonely highway.

Bent and twisted he sat
fashioning handles of hickory
with eyes always centered within
to stare down the pain,
so young to be an ancient
too tired to want anything,
smiling, at last, crookedly,
when death offered its dark robe.

And grandfather's bones stirred
once in mute grief, and made room
for the son he barely knew
and the pain was passed on
    and on
not only to another son,
but to a tribe.

And falling forever
with over and under,
I clutch at naked sky

to stand on firm earth,
    father,
I live you moment by moment.

Crow

back and forth cawings between black,
wet trees and crows, early morning
joyful conversation, a light drizzle
accents the gleam of flapping wings,
    Spring scents the air
in promise of green corn shoots,
and the breeze carries a richness
of thawing soil and "caw"
and answering "caw" lifts my body
upward
    and I flap mightily
to climb above the trees
and look over my shoulder
for one, last, joyous
                "caw".

Storm Mountain Face

Charlie bends to feed the stove
dry oak, and the fire throws
a glow of red in early morning,
I take the pot of coffee and pour
our cups full, and the dog
thumps her tail upon the floor

her nose twitching in sleep
and from the odor of deerhide
soaking in a bucket. I roll
a smoke and we listen to
the steady beat of rain against
the roof and dripping to ground.

"Yes, I was thinking of the drum
we are to make
and trying to dream its shape
and sound, but the images weren't
clear at all, and the rain was
drumming all night, and so I came
over to ask if you'd heard its
shape and sound yet."
                              Charlie
asked this, sipping coffee and
the firebox door was still open
and our shadows were quivering
giants across the floor and walls
and the sharp odor of ripe hide
stung the room, and I hesitated

awhile, remembering a strange dream
mixed with the outdoors through window
earlier visions of the night, of

lightning upright walking the
sagebrush land, electric-charged
walkers become outlines

of bright colored dancing, dancing
acrid puffs of power of feet
to ground, dancing a frenzy
across sand dunes to the west
toward the first low hills
of Storm Mountain, where clouds
of dark waters are born

and reflect themselves in the lake
of a tamarack village up there
in the midst of fir and cedar
where bear and deer wander. "No,
I heard no shape or sound, but
saw a thing, a wonderous, though

frightening, thing. I can't remember
just what it might be, a thought
of my own imagining, or something
I'm to know about later, maybe."
And Charlie looked at the hide
soaking; floating, staring
                              and
beckoned me with a hand.
I leaned toward the bucket
and looked, and then stared:
a shiver sort of at my neck
as I saw the twisted face the
folds of hide portrayed, and:
"yes, I think that's what it
wants to be, and I guess we
have to do it. "And right then

began a frantic pace to do
a thing we didn't know just
what or why, but knew only that
it was ours to do, and
                    don't
thank me hastily, the oak tree
whispered, as I cut slim branches,
and basket willow, too, hoped
I knew what it was all about. And
sapling maple thongs peeled
slippery singing, questioned my

fingers nervous haste, as rain
now slowed to drizzle waiting,
and four hands in a harmony
of expectations began to fashion
a hoop and frame, peeling and
bending and lashing fast with
swift, sure fingers.

then hands again in counter motion
twisting the deerhide to dryness,
the acrid odor dilating nostrils
and racing pulses, forcibly,
as does the blood smell of
freshly killed creatures.

And in a silence of concentration
we lashed the hide to frame
with a coiling lace of maple,
and cut, and inserted fingers
pulling, tearing, forcing
the shape of a face known,
uneven and crude: mouth
curled and open over hide teeth.

Close to fire, the face was leaned,
then we pried open paint cans
and dipped with fingers,
and the face was given a lightning
flash of white, and streaking
dots of blue, and orange lips,

brown earth eye circles and
black night hollow cheeks.

Now long and flowing strands of maple
were tied to frame and knotted,
then hide which was head
of the face we had fashioned
    was completed and
we looked only once, letting it dry
further, close to stove's heat.

We drove to the leveling-off
place of Storm Mountain, close
to tamarack village, beneath an old
fir, there we stood the face, against
the mound of roots and tilted stone,
    and sat beneath a neighbor cedar,
to join the forming storm above
our heads, And maybe walked
about on stabbing lightning legs,
and the black and writhing clouds
were our stomachs in the mind
of storm-thinking, as branches
    whipped in storm dance,
and saplings like grass dance,
heads low to ground, backs arched,
in willing pain,
              the drumming

of rainfingers to shivering branches,
the howling, slapping wind,
                    and
the after calm, and two old men,
bent with age, slowly making
their way down from
                    Storm Mountain.

Red-winged Blackbird

The red-winged blackbird
just now curved
from tree to cattail
clutched there swaying
sideways, head bent
to eye the ground
    in curiosity.

Dandelions bedded
in damp, green grasses,
yawn and stretch
and open themselves
to the sun's warm promise.

At Bald Rock With Old John

"Away down there, yeah,
called Feather River
and across there and downriver
that stone, see?
Where Waktali stood and jumped,
him a land animal become fish.

Then was lots of fish
                    one time
we eat all the time,
                    and deer,
run, walk, all over,
                    deer.

You call loud up here
call very loud it goes,
it goes the voice down
through canyon down,
                    and them,
those ones live in valley,
they hear voice,
                    what you say.
Maybe young girl blush,
                    eh?
Maybe gamblers down there
they laugh,
         laugh and say,
"Oh, that's just Coyote Man
bragging up to Bald Rock."

Sure, I knock down board
throw over stone into brush,
that one guy

he come cut tree
take away to mill
make board
           bring board
stand up here to tell
where trees growing.
      Somebody crazy
so I throw over stone into brush, sure.

Man he come out
to my place,
tell me I live in park,
tell me, "You can't
live in park, belong
to govment, belong to
people."
So I tell him, alright,
I don't live in park
      no more,
I stay my own place.

Yes, my kids
they all get old,
      go away
      maybe die for good,
don't know which.
Me, I don't get old,
                  no
I can't get old
                  no more,
I been around too long.

Reflections on Milkweed

a twisting, turning
flight above, dry
brown grasses
    pods of milkweed seen.

a glimpse of motion
I perceived in journeying
    mind and eye lent joy.

man's art in fingers
lifting to eyes
the silken
    nesting white seedlings

thoughts of white cloud ribs
drifting the vast
blue sky world
    to swallow a star

or the lone seedling
like a bubble
reflecting
    a current of air.

given these moments
to contemplate
and wonder
    a great peace descends.

man's art in thinking
mind-weaving
singular ties
    is but returning.

the seeds within us
and that which
 brought us living
     is an ancient breath.

stone to stone the spark,
fire into dream
into birth,
     we are Creation.

First Light

first light, a dark outline   evening
of a mountain peak and   too
pines their morning scent   will
carried on first breezes,   call,

stars a naked brilliance   to
pulsing to coyote cries   sleep
And keening chorus,   again,

a cricket's tentative chirping,   the
long pauses,   mind
          the fall of an oak leaf   is
a bird's sudden question,   dreaming,

that deepest blue of sky   mind
and now the stars turn   is
brighter,   a
     a sliver of moon   nation
     followed by a star   of
And then first pink of morning   people
sky as vast and open   in
as a child's dreaming,   search,

a carpet of leaves, hazy   mind
grey to mist of yellow   is
the oak growing a cliff face   Creation
reaching out for balance,   space,

a dog bark crawling over a hill,   mind
a snapping conversation of twigs   is
     and branches in fire,   space
I wrap myself in morning   is
     as echos   void

       of a silly dream
linger my mind
and I smile to it,

my urine splashes the ground
sending up an acrid steam,
a long, ribbed cloud I reach for,
    I want to
soar on hawk wings and whistle
an all-consuming pride,

I smell the pine and cedar
and the damp morning soil,
    a flicker calls,
my feet are hooves
I run,
    taking great, soaring
              leaps
above the trees, over hills
to meet
    the sun.

is
crowded
lodge,

mind
is
memory
of
a
way,

a
people
seeking
a
law,
great
law
of
lasting
peace.

Abalone

Yours is the sea,
though torn from life, devoured,
your shell a curiousity, a novelty
to be sold to those who must possess,
to grace a mantle or to receive
dead ashes as a final tribute.

Yours is the sea
I hold your shell to light
to admire the rainbow colors
your body fashioned, the art
of your tribe is a fascination
of wondering if each of you
knew your every design.

All known colors are reflected
like a concave section of universes
      only a dreamer may share,
the rhythm of the sea is felt
and seen are the vast forests
and multitudes of creatures
which inhabit that world.

With coping saw I cut your shell
into large disc landscapes,
and later when I sense contours
and colorings emerging, I curve
my blade to your designs, and
am rewarded with a never-ending
variety of patterns.

I sit upon the frame which supports
a sandstone wheel, a section

of inner tube holding water beneath
the turning wheel, my feet and
legs pumping the wheel to motion,
the music of abrasion, shell on stone
with water, is a lulling sound
and a peaceful feeling ensues.

The outer surface of your shell
turns from grey-green to a brilliance
of all the phases of red,
and when I round the edges
an opaque ivory and silver
lie just beneath the surface.

Now on a hand-turned wheel of cloth
I polish your surfaces,
each so different, seeming to reflect
two universes back to back
which merge in harmony.

As I string your discs, I hope
that the wearer will see to dream
the endless scenes you depict,
and that your beauty be shared
often, and by many,
and that it be remembered
        that yours is the sea.

For Ace

I cannot summon a tear
or feel badly just now,
it's not my loss so much
as it is all our losing.

There won't be a journey to
the pueblo where he was born
or any tracings of childhood
there in red clay dust where
he might have sketched pictures
with a twig,

and no anger at his being taken
from family and home, away
to government school like
so many others.
No one really cares or understands
or even wants to.

He learned to read and to think
and to drink and to smoke dope
and to make love,
just all the usual things,
    except
that he had talent. Wow!
    Imagine that! Talent!

So talented was he that
he was beaten to death
in a Chicago bar.
    Wow! Talent!

So what is it I want to say

or want to remember?
The crazy parties when
we had to help him home,
or the time he was so depressed
at being turned down by a girl?

No, none of these, but all of them,
all the rage, frustration and confusion,
all the love, tenderness and desperation,
all these things which we all carry
within us, but in him
surged with such energy
from brain to fingers to pigment
to living canvas,
                    there, and then,
in those moments I was held,
like a child witnessing first view
of the stars, the frightening,
        wonderous universe.

His energy was overpowering as he
sketched or painted,
I see him standing before a canvas
half as large as the room
buffalo and ghost dancers emerging
alive, moving, demanding more space,
        what'll happen, I wondered in panic,
        when he paints the walls
        and crashes through the window
        and begins painting the streets,
the houses, the billowing clouds,
        the very air?

And his dancers jumped at me
with loud cries, grabbing me,

forcing me into the dance
    and I danced
not gladly, but still frightened
    I danced
    as buffalo pawed earth
and blew and snorted
and blizzards swept the plains,
leaving me a naked, ice-coated tree,
eyes frozen open, forced at last to see.

I danced
        as a nation was slaughtered
and lay broken and bleeding
I danced
        among angered ghosts
who would not lie down gentle
    to death.

I see him at this moment, sketching,
sitting at a littered table,
creating four universes of thought
in as many years,
              fingers in frantic haste
as if tasting the shortness of his life.

I am bitter now, at this moment,
I would reach and pull him from sleep
and make him dance
    with his own dancers,
             with me,
tears streaming down faces
limbs jerking in sanity gone fallen,
and falling into the void of space
we would clutch and grasp at
each and every one of you

and force you into the dance,
and rub your faces into the gore
so proudly you helped create.

And what's the use, and what's the use
my mind screams to the shadows,
so many of our youth
gone into death,
                    so much dying,
and all the blame and blood
and all the justifications
And explanations,
                    add up
to a loss we all share the deed of.
    Yes, it's true,
it is us, the runaways,
the self-made outcasts,
it is to our grief
that we are forgetting
                    the dance.

Road 37C

On a summer's back road
bicycle trip, dodging dogs,
peddling faster to reach
the mirror-vibration asphalt
heat reflected always ahead,
and three black pillars
at road's center, then closer
they become, but can't be,
nuns? holding ritual,
nodding to road to look
at sky and over again, again,
    I slow my approach to enjoy
the momentary mystery, the curious
ways of mind, bending my thoughts
to the occasion, as a flapping
wing and warning "caw" let me
see the reality of three crows
feasting on squished frog
pecking and looking around
so like musicians at an
eternal cocktail party,
or maybe it's a dance
of a cult I cannot know,
    mired in dead frogs I dream
now 3,000 miles later,
remembering that I passed
many dead frogs on that morning
after rain, some with single
leg or arm reaching up or sideways,
and a few snakes, too, and
a live turtle which I
took home and set free
in the backyard river,

and really not any point
to this poem, and won't
ever accuse the crows
who flap heavily by
of resembling nuns
'cause who knows
in what wizard's robe
they walk at night?

Sweetgrass

Sweet rains of summer
remembered in wintertime
in drying sweetgrass.

The fragrance is a sweet warmth
as soft as a blossom's promise
as I early morning huddle
by the woodstove dreaming,
berries ripe there were
scattered in their seasons
on tree and bush and nesting
in grasses tall, waving,
calling in scented voice
to pleasure the day, to dream
undisturbed by outward signs
of traffic or throngs scuttling
to frantic destinations.
And pulling gently, one by one
the long whispers of grass
and hearing frog song and
watching a cattail bending
to the weight of a light question
a red-wing blackbird asks
observing the brilliant passage
of a silent snake, or
the dipping, turning swift
hunger in a swallow's flight.

I add a piece of wood
to the singing of the stove
and drift my mind to feel
again the hot sun on shoulders
the sweat on brow the rich

feel of fertile soil I sink to
upon my knees resting
gathering with mind's fingers
a meadow of grasses
a hillside of forest
a clear brook curving
and widening to reflect
a white roundness of cloud.
  I curve my mind to rhythms
touched and tasted back then
here on winter's shelf
I sort memories and moods
and dwell on yesterday
and all because my body
brushed, in passing,
the bunches of sweetgrass
hanging in winter's house.

Night Room Composition

It begins with closed eyes
and the sizzling of greeen wood
in the stove, sparks popping
tiny questions to the room.
The kettle waits awhile
to join the song, then slowly,
like a far-off insect call,
it joins the composition.
The clock ticks softly
setting the beat, like a drifting
of random thoughts it wanders
in and out of consciousness.
Still with closed eyes
I let mind anticipate
the coming dawn, listening
for the first breeze.
I hear the mouse nibbling
on something borrowed
and smile to think it was
the cat which brought it in.
Puffs of woodsmoke scent
the room, and now the stovepipes
are expanding in heated song
and the music grows faster.
Glancing at the counter
behind the lamp I see
a grouping of figures
wavering in and out of shadow,
a spatula, reflecting night on
burnished surface, the flickering
lamp gives it motion as it
nudges a wooden spoon.
I begin perceiving

things in a new setting,
the march of spice bottles
shoulder to shoulder,
in a far away other corner
an unlit lamp borrows light
to reflect tiny points of fire
like far-off stars.
    A chair with leaning back
seems stretched in relief
remembering a body's weight.
The fat sugarbowl glows
    in a satisfied manner
and poses, like a short, fat
man about to tell one
from the belly.
    A carving in a corner
has lost all dimension
and thus gained for itself
space and depth unlimited.
    A basket suspended
from a rafter offers
mysterious possibilities
in its vast, dark interior.
    It could last forever
and does, of itself as
I close my eyes again
to listen to night room music.

Tsier

The stove expands itself to contain
A new fire built on embers,
an oak knot crackling, the singing
of heated metal,
        the wind
in gusts as if pursuing
its own whispering,
        and he
waits quietly sitting
until the coffee water boils
And the first sip is gulped, scalding,
rocking back and forth a bit
and pausing to feed the fire
to dim the lamp to darkness
of shadows touching one the other,
and the brief flare of a match
catches the first puff of smoke
from his pipe,
        then he leans
back in the rocker, his eyes
gazing at the cobwebbed circle
of ceiling the lamp discloses.
    He rubs
thumb to horn-ridged finger
as if to help his thinking,
and the thought is a picture
without motion, of the woodpile
measured in seasons instead of cords.
The axe hangs on the wall,
his fingers curve the handle's
    shape, he signs,
sipping again, and knowing that today
will be like all the others,

Alone,
solitary
steady
in
life.
There
were
flowers
and
children,
there
was
singing
and
love
once,
once
a
love
so
strong
that
all
else
was
as
nothing.
Gone
all
gone
into
memories,
alone

the bite of axe, the steady
feast of the saw.

sitting,
alone.

Expedition

Lizards leap aside and go panic-crashing
through the dry underbrush, their bodies
lumbering, tails whipping
    as the great wheels
of a monstrous vehicle round the bend
cutting deep furrows in silent dust.
Great clouds swirling in storms
created by the wheels, and by
huge, booted feet which follow in
the wake of the vehicle. And the cat,
a grey mass of furred and fiery
strength, restlessly scouts the trail,
now ahead, now behind, yellow eyes
constantly casting about for signs
of danger, shoulder muscles rippling
tail twitching, apprehensive, alert.
    The sudden, shrill cry
of a bird overhead, then the flapping
of desperate wings seeking freedom.
The wheels of the monstrous vehicle
slow and stop, for just ahead,
not moving, legs braced to earth
as if to challenge the very sky
is a great, black-domed insect
glistening through the clouds of dust.
    The vehicle pauses momentarily,
then slowly approaches the
waiting insect. Another lizard
unseen, suddenly breaks and crashes
for safety. The cat pounces,
too late, for the reptile is gone.
Tail twitching in agitation,
the cat approaches the insect

and eyes it doubtfully.
   My son leans forward on
his tricycle to study the stinkbug,
then turns to slowly climb
the ridge at road's center,
      as we continue our journey.

Sculpture in Soil

What fire has blackened to sleeping
the earth her breath of green now sings,
and the flanks and belly of these hills
are stroked by fingers roughened
        in the sculpture of labor.
What seeds which slept so long in dreaming
the sun and soil have called to dance,
and winds that once were grey with ash
now sway the seedlings in their nests,
        balanced on tiny, probing feet.
The early summer children run about
on long and awkward legs of grace,
and trembling hooves of song are felt
by those who kneel to touch the soil
        while placing seeds in furrows warm.
At evening's campfire when stars appear
and crickets and frogs chorus the moon,
cast in shadows of dark granite, I see
the walking sculptures which guard night
        and gentle our bodies to sleeping.

Dedication of a Roundhouse

Bent and twisted by many seasons
bowed like the ancient oak close by
walking slowly on swollen feet and ankles
her eyes whitened by time
                              painfully
she unravels the kerchief
and pours her offering
at the base of the center pole.

The grey smoke curls upward
like hair being braided to the sky
and the faces in the circle
of the roundhouse
are silent carvings
fashioned by fire.

The pit drum pulses
earth her heartbeat
as shadows quiver and face
themselves upon the rounded wall.

A singer sends forth a plea
his voice becoming dancers' feet,
then I see the old one smile
as if the puffs of dust
were reliving all her seasons.

And rattlesnake and dry, wind-blown leaves
are the voice of elderberry clapper,
and every bird or other
gentle sound that ever was
is retold by the dancers' whistles.
And the sounds and visions are one

with smoke and sky dreaming,
night warmth sighs the grasses,
and the oaks downslope whisper
their content that the people
   are returned.

In quiet wonder at this feast
I trail my thoughts in dust
unwinding recorded history
like leaves plucked by wind.

Dogwood Blossoms

It's a question of bright stars
and of four petals cupped
to catch sun and reflect
a hovering circle of white.

Here, where the big trees
were so recently logged-off
and the jagged teeth of stumps
and broken arms of branches
question the meaning of sanity.

A slide of mud and stones
advances down the ravine,
and dogwood and maple are bowed
under weight of future burial.

It's a question of the last act
before a man-made dying
that hundreds of blossoms
shout a final triumph
for earth and sky to behold.

Were we to be an armless,
legless race of creatures
belly-crawling through life
perhaps we could learn of beauty,

but instead we cut down
the very answers we seek
in torn earth, and the secrets
remain unseen by us, as we
plunge forward blindly,
        brushing aside blossoms.

Earth And Creation

He held the drum up
to the heat of
morning sun,
    and the sound was Earth.

She held the child high
to breath the
air of morning,
    and heard Creation.

Sandhills That None May Visit

Sandhills that none may visit,
crumbled ruins which echo a song
carried on the winds of yesterday.
A lone coyote keening the moon,
the headlights of a car
    searching through the night.
The silent laughter of stars
as they dance their light
across an endless landscape.

Each daylight rises, a praise
in the song of Creation.
A circle of drummers and singers
gathered low upon a sandhill,
and the eagerness of ourselves
in a running stagger through sand
to join their circle.
              And they
keep fading back into distance,
and their music is like a memory,
as we become shadows of tomorrow
on the red stone cliffs of today.

Springtime flowers born of snow,
crystals floating on a desert wind.
A sacred message etched in sand,
magic tumbling track of sidewinder.
At the corner of the eye, naked stone,
and lightning dancers leaping from
black, rumbling storm clouds.

A large track no one recognizes
    behind us

slowly filling with sand.
Sudden laughter where
    only emptiness was.

A lizard transfixed upon a stone
waiting into forever,
                as we
do push-ups and grow tails.

Dried, scattered corn stalks
rustling in the desert wind
    as an old man
shakes a gourd rattle and chants,
his eyes closed, a smile playing
games of youth.

A woman on her knees, patting
soft circles of frybread
    as a child
watches her, and then solemnly
says, "I'm going to be a dancer."
And the woman looks back
at the child as solemnly
and says, "Yes, you will be a dancer."

A piece of pottery, smooth and
rounded by fingers of wind,
the same wind whose flute
plays the cottonwood's
    Creation song.

We pass our own scattered bones
lying in jagged fragments,
home for scorpions, and we
smile at those brittle memories,

crumbling them between fingers.

And we pause at a waterhole
to study the countless markings,
and drink deeply, to become rivers,
and lie back upon the sand
and stretch out, and out,
as our bodies become mountains
and crumble into sandhills
that none may visit.

A Fallen Oak

the great, gnarled fingers of roots
have torn free of the granite base,
protector of bedrock mortars
now exposed.
              See, the old
fallen one seems to say,
before my birth there
were a people here
who ground the seedlings
of my ancestors for food
      back then
so long ago when there
was the giving of shade
and the praise and wonder
to saplings.
              Now
cut me up and
heat the life of your house
and think of me
in warm dreaming,
then spread my ashes thin
beneath my offspring.
      Yes,
there were a people here
      once,
              and if ever
you should meet them
tell them that
I waited
              a long time.

The old man's lazy,

I heard the Indian Agent say,
has no pride, no get up
and go. Well, he came out
here and walked around my
place, that agent. Steps
all through the milkweed and
curing wormwood; tells me
my place is overgrown
and should be made use
of.

The old split cedar
fence stands at many
angles, and much of it
lies on the ground like
a curving sentence of
stick writing. An old
language, too, black with
age, with different
shades of green of moss
and lichen.
       He always
says he understands us
Indians,
          and why don't
I fix the fence at least;
so I took some fine
hawk feathers fixed
to a miniature woven
shield
       and hung this
from an upright post
near the house.

He
came by last week
and looked all around
again, eyed the feathers
for a long time.

                    He didn't
say anything, and he didn't
smile even, or look within
himself for the hawk.

Maybe sometime I'll
tell him that the fence
isn't mine to begin with,
but was put up by
the white guy who used
to live next door.

                    It was
years ago. He built a cabin,
then put up the fence. He
only looked at me once,
after his fence was up,
he nodded at me as if
to show that he knew I
was here, I guess.

                    It was
a pretty fence, enclosing
that guy, and I felt lucky
to be on the outside
of it.
          Well, that guy
dug holes all over his
place, looking for gold,

and I guess
            he never
found any. I watched
him grow old for over
twenty years, and bitter,
I could feel his anger
all over the place.
That's when I took to
leaving my place to do
a lot of visiting.
            Then
one time I came home
and knew he was gone
for good.

My children would
always ask me why I
didn't move to town
and be closer to them.

Now, they
tell me I'm lucky to be
living way out here.
            And
they bring their children
and come out and visit me,
and I can feel that they
want to live out here
too, but can't
for some reason, do it.

Each day
a different story is
told me by the fence,
the rain and wind and snow,

the sun and moon and shadows,
this wonderful earth,
     this Creation.
I tell my grandchildren
many of these stories,
     perhaps
this too is one of them.

Old Tom would tell us

the fire looked real good,
standing at the entrance
to Coyote's Roundhouse.
　　He'd stoop to enter,
leaning his age on
his walking stick.
　　　　　　Always,
he'd circle the room,
and center pole, and sit
close to the pole.
　　　　　　Raising
his head, he'd look through
the smoke hole, at the stars,
then nod his head, yes.
　　Then he'd look around
the circle of faces
and maybe wink
And clear his throat,
and begin:
　　　　　　"One time
Coyote was sitting
in the sweat house
　　when he heard
a noise outside."
　　And Tom
would smile and maybe
laugh, remembering
　　　　　　Coyote.
　　And sometimes
we had to wait
a long, long time
for the story
　　　　　to continue.

127

Grandma Marie Potts

She was grandma to everyone,
even us older people.
When she came to
the Bear Dance, we would
all crowd around her car
to welcome her.
　She'd cock her head
at an old timer
and say something in Maidu
and they'd have
a fast back and forth
then both
burst into laughter.
　She'd only rest
a short time in the house
then begin
asking questions
which were
directions for setting
the camp in order.
　Children gathering
firewood and carrying
water, women
and girls
already cooking,
the men
starting to butcher
and lighting the fire
in the roasting pit.
　Tents
would be going up
for two days,
children

all over the place.
　　At sunrise ceremony
she stood
dressed in doeskin
holding
a bright flicker band.

And that's how I see her
now.
　　And when
she passed away,
we all of us hurt
for a long time.
　　And I wonder
if others saw
what I did:
　　the great grandchildren
dancing,
　　　　grandma's eyes
looking
　　　　from them.

Incense

Cold, sharp and very lean, the wind
bends itself around the house.
The last scurrying oak leaves
roll their dry-edged sound downslope.
The stars are brilliant ice crystals
hanging from the roof of the world.
A scent from cedar kindling
has wakened a memory of
a long ago gift of incense from
Mexico, made of corn meal,
husks, and pine pitch.
And like the wind, I bend
my thoughts in curve to explore
other places and times.
It was a small fire of
greasewood and sage, out there
in dunes close by a spring
in the heart of a desert valley.
Sitting, breaking branches to feed
my small fire, sand blowing,
I saw the process of moving dunes.
My eyes were closed to slits,
full of sand, a kerchief covered
my mouth. I blinked, once,
and across the fire from me,
sitting on his heels was a man,
old and naked, breaking branches
and carefully putting them
upon the fire, all the while
staring into my eyes. No emotion
at all, it was as if he were
waiting for me to make my move.
I stared back at him, myself

waiting. And when I had
to blink again, he was gone.
   But never really gone, for I
still see him at quiet times
in my mind, staring at me, waiting.
And since then I feel that
he was merely letting me know
that he was still here,
and that all of his relatives,
and mine, too, were waiting.
   A fire of juniper branches
now enters my thoughts.
Camped upon a ridge between
mountains, boiling a tin of
water for coffee. A clatter
of small stones dislodged
behind me. I sat, not moving.
Maybe I would see a bighorn
sheep, I was hoping, waiting.
No other sound came and still
I did not move. I became dawn
and that first breeze was myself,
knowing, in the light of self,
that someone was watching me
from the rocks above and behind.
I packed my gear at sunrise
and began walking, never looking
back, and I've often wondered
since then if I should have
climbed, climbed to the source
of that sound of falling stones.
   So many circles of ashes
in this land, some covered,
some blown away, by other winds.
So many campfires at this moment,

scattered across this great land,
like the oak leaves outside
this window.

And the promises
sent to sky in smoke
of cedar, sage, willow,
juniper, and all the other
sacred plants.

And the someone
who always watches.

Deeper Than a Dream

(for oboe)

like a memory beyond death
I awake to find myself become
a mass of obsidian far underground,
having witnessed light only once
and briefly, I retain that light
at the core of my being,
                              brighter
than any remembered sun.
    A thought intruded:
"Can a mass of obsidian
have being?" And the
thought caused a fracture
which shook the western
edge of a continent.
    Now, when I surface,
an earthworm will worry
a tunnel through the fracture
and thus will begin
my disintegration,
                    I thought,
settling down to
    further centuries.

A Gentle Earthquake

(for Mt. St. Helens)

An all night summer wind, hot   Once
and dry without a hint of seas.   a
A restless tossing, turning series   feast
of short-lived dreams set mind   was
to rhythms of remembered oceans.   given
A rolling shiver of earth skin   and
shakes the vessel of this sleeping house,   every-
and caught between dream and awakening.   one
I wait for the next slight tremor.   ate.

Mama Coyote and her two pups   Once
respond to the earthquake in song   a
as if having known and sat the night   song
awaiting their cue, and a bird, too,   was
cheeps a short, shrill, many-sided   sung
note, joining the keening barks.   in
The dry, brown grasses bend to   praise.
the slight increase in wind, as   of
crickets one by one begin again   all.

their chorus of song. (And if restless,   Once
you may, like me, untangle yourself   a
from twisted sheets to dress in darkness   drum
and in darkness go outdoors to stand   was
and breathe of grass-scented wind   pulse
and raise face to sky and suck   to
in breath, astonished that such   the
a vast and brilliant display of   all-
stars keep happening into eternity).   ness.

Quickly forgotten dreams, dropped to   Once

earth, as star fingers which are
thoughts, pluck nerve ends to
further expand the universal wheel,
and the crickets, too, rejoice and
grow their song among invisible
grasses which are seas which
reflect the song in star pictures
floating upon an endless ocean.

An earthquake is not a devastation,
a malicious act of nature against man.
An earthquake is because it must be.
The early morning newsperson reports
minor damage here and there. He does
not declare a state of emergency. He
does not suggest a praise to earth
her wonderous breath of life

so freely given. Yes, ah, yes, it
takes humanity, pencil, and paper,
to sit as I commenting on events. Now,
this short time later, I fashion
a parchment of green oak leaves
against a blue sky, take up
a brush of soaproot buried deep,
and for pigment mix my sweat

with tobacco juice left by grasshopper,
white foam spit of frog, cupped
dewdrops from varied flowers,
a touch of robin "cheer-up",
a faint trace of coyote barkings,
and mix this delicate pigment
in the hollow vessel of a concave
thought, and begin to paint

a
people
lived
in
balance
with
Crea-
tion.

The
sky
is
a
feast
of
stars
which

are
drum
beats
in
a
song
return-
ing.

A
rattle
is
an
earth-
quake
shak-
ing.

a landscape/dreamscape/
furturescape/mindscape, dwelling
on cloud-thoughts soon to be
evaporated over countless seas;
ribs of rainbows, skulls of boulders
shrewn over a granite base of
bedrock reflecting glaciers
given once in yesterday.

A
bull-
roarer
is
wind
force
call-
ing.

    I sit upon stone hill, a mile
above a green and winding river.
Upon the trail I'd encountered
old cedar posts leaning, some
lying lichen-coated upon leaves.
Small metal tags hammered into
trees porclaim BLM or private

A
flute
is
all
life
sing-
ing.

ownership. I think of crumbled
villages of stone far to the south,
of cobble pictures in the sand
just across these high sierras.
I suck in breath and pull a drink
from the river far below, trying
to ignore the one-man dredge

Light-
ning
is
masked
dancer
in-
viting

whining its greed as it sucks-up
sand and pebbles searching for gold.
I embarrass myself with a sob
which wracks my body just once,
brought on by mind's fingers
dipping into the away down there
river, and asking again, again:

us
to
join
the
round
dance
tonight.

Who guards your waters now?
And these beautiful bluffs and

Fire
is

forested hills: who are the guardians,
who, indeed are the guardians of
this good earth? Surely not us!
Guardianship which is Creation's song
no longer issues from our lips.

    Is it possible to shout back the praise
which was given us once in a long ago
yesterday? To dream back the dreamers?
There is a metal tag nailed to my
forehead, and it says, BLM. There is
barbwire wrapped around my wrists.

How did it come to be that we
gave over the power of Creation's
balance to government agencies and
corporations bent on destruction?
It is much like sending yourself as
a child, to government boarding school.

The old parchments of law are brittle,
and because they had to be written
down and re-read for enlightenment,
there, under glass, they cannot
.even become the compost they
were surely meant to be.

The Great Law of Peace of
the Six Nations is a beginning:
it is a lifeway memorized and
recited to the people. Memory is
knowing, mind is Creation space:
mind is, we are, Creation dreaming.

    The lands of earth are floating plates,

a
call
to
feast.
Water
is
sur-
round-
ing
us
all.
The
sen-
tence
of
a
snake
trail
in
sand,
a
fish
float-
ing
in
its
own
space,
a
bird

137

the scientists now say. The Huichol have
a story of Coyote biting turtle and
shattering her shell, and when he
did so, World Pond dried-up, dying.

It took all of the creatures of earth
and the memory of turtle and water
to sing a plea to Coyote to please
regurgitate the allness of turtle,
and when he did so: water was.

Is it greed to call ourselves
people creatures of turtle island?
Can it be that turtle is still
shattered, and is more than a
continent, more than mere imagination?

An ancient people are those
who remember an original
promise. I meditate upon the
rhythm of a shovel at work,
I ponder the earthworm in wonder.

   Volcanic ash is floating to fall
all over earth, covering combustible
rivers, polluted lakes, nuclear plants,
in a soft blanket of warning.

An old Hopi is hoeing his cornfield.
A Mohawk village is surrounded
by armed troops. A Cree is
spearing fish which will slowly

poison his own loved family.
On the other side of earth

sings
us
"ah-
waken"

Seeds
of
corn
fall-
ing,

green
beans
ripen-
ing,
fat

squash
and
melons
tempt-
ing,

rain
fall-
ing
rain.

Sun
warm-
ing
sun.

Night
sleep-

a shaman on a high plateau
is praising the dawn. Her song

stirs the leaves outside my window,
her shadow is a cloud passing by,
she is a warm breath of wind
which soothes my sleeping children.

   On the other side of earth
and south, a painted human
twirls a bull-roarer and the sound

pauses momentarily, as earth
searches for her missing nations.
   An eagle wheels the sun.

Between two oceans, I hear the
scraping of my grandfather's hoe,
an echo of thirty years returned.

An unborn child whimpers in sleep,
a fawn staggers to stand on
trembling legs, as ears twitch in

   wonder. Again earth skin
rolling, nodding stars. Now

the voices murmur close by,
all the ancients are returned.

Our small existence is reflected
on the underbelly of a tortoise,

waves of coral light shadows
in this World Pond, dreaming.

ing
night.

Green
sprouts
from
earth,

tend-
er
green.

Hands
cupped
to

drink
clear
water,

water
emerg-
ing

from
ground

water
liv-

ing
in

sky,
water

A sea of waving grasses   con-

hooves of extinct creatures   tain-

ourselves in exile, and always   ing

   a forgiving earth.   Earth.

Pomo Basketmaker

Her gnarled, brown fingers
fashion constellations
circling oceans.
The tidal pull of
her basket's center
is heart to many nations.
Willow ribs
fanning all directions
the tips of which,
like firefly spirits,
call to a people
that all is
ever was
an upturned basket.

Chokecherries

Clusters which invite the morning sun,
a deep red richness on a backdrop
of dark green leaves. Only a child
can truly know the taste, an eyes-
closed tartness which coats the tongue
like raspings from a sapling spruce.

Not a house in sight, in this scene:
a winding stream, a green of tall grasses,
two swallows praising air, a single,
startled frog croak which introduces
a tiny face peering from behind
the huge globe of giant puffball.

And together, child and little person
sit silent as they exchange stories
created within the vast landscape
of a youthful Creation. Flute players
appear who are walking nations
re-discovering their own true meanings.

Will I break the spell of peace if I
dare to sit beside them? Will I be
welcome to this feast of dreams?
I approach and gaze down at myself,
a child asleep beside a stream,
clusters of chokecherries overhead.

Hobo Bird

Nanao and myself at the pond,
by the pond, close to it, in
it, reflected there beneath
pines.

Dawn's first birds bathe,
fluttering tiny, winged
bodies, creating ripples
which

spread in circle to encompass
the wheeling universe.
                    A doe
and fawn drink.

We sit for many lifetimes,
silently watching.
                    The retreat
bell just up the hill

breaks morning like a
religious fart. We are
forced into now time.
Nanao cocks his head

so like the words he is
about to speak:
    "I, Hobo Bird!"
He says. Yes, Nanao,
you are Hobo Bird.

    This new pond!
Nanao jumps in,
    no ripples, nothing.

A Meditation of Leaves

a crisp, curling invitation
to silent drift of clouds
high above.
        A singular cricket
chirp in December.
           A wind
gusting suddenly to swirl
the leaves in tumbling play,
to touch and become part
of an updraft, a vertical
wall of fluttering leaf bats,
up and around, and around
and aground, fallen.
    And the oak tree
leans, bends and sends
arms and fingers of branches
as if to clutch lost children.
    Then rain a slanting
come rushing music heard
as breast down of winter
settles upon this roof.

    A sleep of ocean waves
come to these far-off
mountain foothills, rain
drumming a sharp angle
upon a metal roof,
           creating
a turbulence of dreaming
like driftwood cast upon
a far away, long forgotten
shore.
    A between-dreams

awakening, tentatively
                lent
to light a lamp of thought
in this cobwebbed house.

I kindle myself to flame
close by the woodstove,
    crumpled bat wings
    encase the self of me
that winter has given me
    for a robe.

I surround myself
in woodsmoke wonder
    and warmth,
here at Nightbird Camp.

For a Dog-killed Doe

They say she cried her agony for a long time
as dog fangs tore her body apart,
                             trapped
at the corner of a fence, too swollen with
an unborn fawn to leap and run any further.

The neighbor took her in a wheelbarrow,
ready to take her body outside the fence
and dump her in a gully. "She's no more
good," he said, not looking at me.

"She's still alright," I said, meaning
much more as I looked into her eyes,
still so alive-seeming.
                    There were two
deaths standing close by.

                 When I cut
her belly open, that which was dead
tumbled out as if to mimic birth.
Many nations passed through my mind
as I began skinning the body of her clan.

I sit eating the flesh of her youth,
taking the strength of her never-to-be
motherhood. I feast solemnly,
                      wishing
sadly that I could take her back
   to winter.

Within The Seasons

winter solstice

When darkness settles itself
upon blanket of crystal snow
and stars are like piercing thoughts
of reason in the mind of Creation,
    we bank the hearth's fire, that
morning finds the children warm.

We taste last summer's gifts
of corn and beans and squash.
At winter's table we give thanks
and praise Creation in quiet song,
    then we too settle beneath robes
to dream the promise of tomorrow.

On a morning so brilliant that
blood stirs the children to noisy play,
the maples call to us in rising sap
and a whole nation responds.
    Nothing else quite so festive as
the all night fires of a sugar camp.

spring equinox

Now day and night sit balanced.
From a silence that seemed forever,
the first booming crash of break-up
thunders from the river. Smiling,
    an elder oils the handle of a hoe
and listens for that great, warm wind.

Creation is a song, a trickling become

a gurgling, chuckling water voice.
Winds which bend the snows to melting
carry clouds of rain storms on shoulders.
    Green islands appear on turtle's back
grasses long asleep beneath the snow.

Dawn of a glorious season, flowers
in merging, undulating waves of color.
The taste of strawberries, anticipated
in their blossoms, the rich and fertile
    smells of soil we bend to,
breaking the ground for summer's corn.

summer solstice

Come, bring the children. Let them
feel for a moment the rhythm
of the hoe. Let them experience
the wonder of green shoots emerging
    from earth, earth given us
in guardianship from the Creation.

Body, mind, and spirit full to bursting
with ripe, sweet berries, the first
tender green beans, and corn. We give
thanks, and thanks again. The twin
    concepts of Reason and Peace are
seen in each kernel of an ear of corn.

Perhaps we repair our lodges
as do the beavers living close by.
Our children swim like river otters
and as their laughter reaches us,
    we join them for a while
in these hottest of summer days.

autumn equinox

Again, day and night sit balanced
and the black bear begins to put on fat.
We begin harvesting mature crops
to store for winter. Our elders
     choose and carefully store away
the seeds to be planted in tomorrow.

That sacred song of departure,
dry cornstalks rustling in wind.
At their feet huge, fat pumpkins.
Above us, the sky darkens with
     a great passage of birds.
Again, we pause to give thanks.

Wood piled high close to lodges,
we walk upon crackling, brown,
frozen grasses. Evening calls to us,
softly, in gentle song. And soon
     the first large flakes of snow
call us to rest beneath winter's robe.

Crow's Flight

I watched the solitary flight
of a black and silent crow,
never a sound, not looking around,
bent upon a one-way flight
heading toward the edge of night.

Searching for Eagles

A pair of great blue herons should
be feast enough for anyone's sunset.
Still, I chant an inner prayer
to glimpse but once, a circling,
soaring eagle close to
this river at my doorstep.

This bit of Mohawk territory, encircled
by cities, towns, freeway and seaway,
cannot be what my ancestors dreamed.
They, who intimately knew eagles,
how would they reconcile today
without the loon's evening cry?

I pretend this river at my doorstep,
for it is a backwash of the seaway,
not flowing, but pulled back and forth
by passing ships. No more the taste
of fresh fish, what swim here are
sickly, polluted, and dying creatures.

Few stars penetrate the man-made
haze of light. No owls hoot the night.
What may resemble peaceful sleep
is the reaction to troubled reality.
No, no more eagles soar here, only
those kept harbored deep within.

Quebec, rattling chains of Separatism

unaware that the links of a continent
are the backbones of mountains,
the veins of rivers, and the fertile
    belly of flatlands.

James Bay is in guardianship to
the true natives, Mr. and Mrs. Hydrabec.
The only true distinction you and yours
ever possessed was greed and the
    inability to see tomorrow.

The Born-Again Ice Age is descending
upon the brows of politicians.
This new winter of discontent
will incubate a multitude
    of the newly curious.

It is already written by fingers of ice
upon the walls of Parliament,
that a new leadership is wanted,
a completely new way of perceiving
    the reality of this vast land.

This continent was never a fatherland.
This land is a bursting pregnancy
of energy and new life, ever
eager to spring forth to protect
    and cherish the clan mothers

of the countless creatures and creations
which abound upon her landscape.
Soon, everyone will open their minds
to the screaming eagle, and
    the quiet of turtle.

Reflections on the St. Lawrence Seaway

Ships that pass in the night
    do so often before
my front window, calling
    out prehistoric challenges
just before their lighted
    bodies pass through
one another, like mirages
    meeting in a dream
leaving wakes of undulations
    dark, synthetic storms
which toss violent waves
    against the seawall.

These man-made tempests are
    fictions written by machines,
as are the seawalls, gouged out
    of naked granite and slate
to fashion this stagnant sewer
    of zebra mussel beds and other
filthy matter brought to us
    by foreign thought and deed
to lend temporary wealth to
    those who dare not dream
of possible tomorrows based
    upon their own generosity.

Ships that pass in the night
    are reflections of modern man
resting only to feast upon
    the resources of this earth,
then quickly moving on, seeking
    further tribute from any of

the floating plates of land upon
this planet once held sacred,
envisioning riches even there
among the very stars, as they
plunder and rape their only source
of sustenance and possible peace.

They would all grow rich today
and fatten egos and purses at
the expense of their own children.
But tomorrow will not take care
of itelf, as once was thought.
And when men finally disappear,
taking countless species with them,
the earth will continue her trip
among the galaxies, perhaps wondering
just what went wrong with that
short-lived species, Man, which
threw away the gift of life.

Brief History (June-December 1994)

Last summer a tiny spider wove
a miniature web of delicate silk
beneath the porch rail at the meeting
place of braces and upright, angled.
From this hidden lair, I watched
a ballet of the hunt, surreal, for
nothing seemed vicious or cruel,
merely a continuation of dance.

> *That morning's news brought scenes*
> *of mangled flesh in Sarajevo, of a*
> *child sitting rocking back and forth,*
> *hugging herself and staring at us.*

> *An elder much like our grandparents*
> *shuffled slowly, plastic bottle in hand*
> *seeking water and bits of wood to burn,*
> *a desperate hope held, but waning.*

A slightly larger spider arrived
to occupy an opposite position
and the two went about their hunts
as if unaware of one another.
Then suddenly the larger spider darted
around the upright to devour the lesser
and tore apart the miniature web
as if to erase all claims in future.

> *An unending throng, in despair flee*
> *their birthplace, Rawanda, hopelessly*
> *reaching with hands and eyes to cameras*
> *recording their misery and doom.*

> *A child is trampled beneath the*
> *feet of relatives who cannot see*
> *beyond the horrors just experienced*
> *in this madness of ethnic hate.*

By summer's end many spiders had
lived their short lives there beneath
the porch rail, each larger and bolder
than the last, seeking only reproduction.
   I thought of Darwin. Could it be
that survival is indeed the end game?
But no, for with each season to be
the tiny spider will reappear
       I had a childhood friend who knew
       no living elders in his family, for
       they had been taken to death by
       those who hate for the sake of hatred.
       He grew to manhood yearning for
       a past he can never know, often
       wondering what it must be like to
       hear the wisdom of grandparents.

Silken cocoons cling there, where
spiders had competed for space
and if worm and weather allow
they may relearn new seasons.
   In winter dreaming, surely
violence is a factor unknown
and thoughts a manifestation
of Creation's wondrous cycle.
       In the mid-Eurasian continent
       death is a walking presence, taking
       at random the child and elder
       like an every-expanding plague.
       Who hold the gun proclaim law!
       Too often it seems that ideals,
       like limbs, can be severed to
       separate body from sane thought.

Gift of Stone

Once upon a sandy beach
miniature dunes etched by wind
were a written record of waters
    a half mile distant.

A trickle from a nearby mountain
was mother to a grove of willows
which dry-clattered their branches
    for most of each year.

A terrible stench permeated all
within this shaded stand, the putrid
odors of creatures whose task
    is devouring the dead.

These feared-by-many vultures
brood and belch here, communicating
by scent, flapping heavily away
    when summoned by death.

At the edge of this haven, circling
to avoid its foulness, I saw
lying in the sand like an offering
    a carefully crafted stone.

A weight, designed to absorb water
and sink nets in this desert lake,
perhaps detached and lost here
    when this was an inland sea.

I carried it in awe and respect,
this treasure given only once,
to drop into deep blue waters

returning the gift to the giver.

I raised my eyes to the mountains
and studied ancient beach lines
hundreds of feet above, standing
    there beneath a former sea.

I thanked the vultures for detouring
my steps. I thanked the rains for
nourishing the lake. I thanked the
    hands which fashioned the gift.

I built a small fire and spent
the night star-gazing, in wonder
that the vast universe can be
    mirrored in a silent lake.

Old Friends

Dark-Buffalo, are you out on the plains
in a rusty pickup, still counting
the holes in your old boots?
You were always laughing and promising
to sing me your special vision song.
But you never did, and I suspect that
your laughter was the true vision.

And you, Painted-Hand, growing old
behind steel bars for defending
women and children, I know that
you haven't forgotten the desert
sands you introduced me to, the
mountains, always ahead.

And, Feather-Held, did you ever
return to the far north to marry
that "big clumsy guy" you used to
tell me about? The way you smiled
when you spoke of him is the way
every man would wish to know
at least once in his lifetime.

And You-I-cannot-name because
your name has already been re-given,
you died so quickly. And when
we reached you, you were smiling.
Your blood still stains this ground,
for the years can never erase
one who dies for a people.

My friends, as heavy rain falls
I just wanted to remember you all.

Hurricane Andrew

Awesome in beauty, spinning
in counter-clockwise motion,
a galaxy newly born
replicating ancestors.

That man chose to depict
such wonder as personal
is a meager message of
self, bloated beyond vision.

True destruction in overkill
is over-exploitation
of earth-given resources
lent us as a gift but once.

To recognize the power
of earthquakes and tornados,
in beauty, is the balance
Creation seeks to portray.

Backward Dancer

"Anger? Do you wish to see anger?" I
shouted, dancing backward, backward
dancing around the firepit, singeing
ankles and toes in pain-seeking pleasure,
stomping sparks and ashes in imitation of
that final earthquake. And corn husks

rattled where no wind stirred. Voices
grunted, groaned from elmbark walls,
faces appeared which were masks twisted
and drooling an acrid, yellow bile.
Rattles spoke in shattering hailstorms
as I became an ice-coated dancer

    reaching for that so easily reached
    upon the longhouse wall, vague
    rifle shape given flickering motion
    by an angry fire of thorns, of ice.

"Anger? You wish for anger?" Again shouting,
as my backward dance becomes a sliver dance
of piercing ice crystals. And the hundred masks
which are pure rage puff out their cheeks
to blow a hurricane upon my dancing,
and at last, arms reaching for that final

flame, I fall to earth dying, my hands
buried in embers, my mind at last entering
into that final sleep.
               And "Unh!" and "Unh!"
as my long-departed father pulls me from,
drags me from that flesh-cooking fire.

And above me, hovering, sharp reality of
a rifle from which hangs feathers,
yours and mine to take in hate or
take as an offering to the people.

Disembodied, unthinking, I sit beside
a whispering fire of birch, holding before
my eyes two hands carved of red cedar,
enormous hands without articulation. And
opposite sits my father staring into my eyes,
all the pain that ever was, marked in

deep creases upon his face in death.
He sprinkles sweetgrass and sage upon
the fire. He is humming to himself a song
he once sang to rock my cradle board.
And behind him, smiling, my grandfather
stands with hand upon the shoulder of

his son, my father. And his
other hand holds loosely a rifle,
and he, too, stares into my eyes
questioning the meaning of my existence.

Then father stands, and they approach me
from opposite sides of the fire.
Nothing is gentle in their touch as
they rub my body with oils, rub
until I am a tingling object of
burning pain. And my hands they

take one each to hold close to
their mouths as they puff out
cheeks and become two false-face
masks blowing on my hands. "Your

heart is a cold, blue crystal." So
says the turtle rattle shushing me

a final warning. And waterdrum sings
a singular note which fractures my
crystal heart.
The shards melt to

become one. Warmth enters the
hollow of my heart's cavity. Then I
become a flowing wisp of smoke
curling around the longhouse walls. Now,
I, too, am a mask of twisted countenance,
a message in the mirror of self. As

a multitude of masks crowd my being
and send their ancient thoughts to me,
I become one: a nation. And vague
rifle shape beside me there dances,
backward dances an echo of the me
that was and is no more. I close

my wooden eyes and clasp dry
fingers which are paws, as I
become another beginning, another
chant in the cycle of the Creation.

From the mind of Creation was given
a question: "Who will bury
tomorrow's children?" I'd become
a red cedar meditation, and as such
searched my mind and heart for many
eternities. And I watched all species

of this good earth fulfill their promise.

And the answer came to me from then and now,
that, "No! I will dig no graves to
sleep my children in death. Let all
that ever was and will, be their
gift from us, their parents."

And rattle and waterdrum became
the songs of all seasons to come.
And when at last I lay down
to that final sleep, I was born
   a nation.

Being Forever

At the rim of sunset waters
far across this great island
where mountains slant
into salt ocean
    at land's end,
on a hillside there
among giant redwoods
coyote cries the moon,
on a hillside there
where breezes scent air
with sage and cedar
and red-tail hawk rides
currents of cool air,

alone there in waiting
a roundhouse of cedar
merges hill and forest,
and softly in silence
large snowflakes fall.

And snow falls here
at morning's sun
and trees their boughs
bend heavy in sleep
close by the longhouse.

It is corn hung on rafters
to dry, or storage baskets
full of acorn and pinenuts,
it is squash and beans
or smoked salmon and eel,
juniper smoke curling
from adobe village

high atop a mesa.

It is the hunter poised
at breathing hole of seal
and dugout gliding
    a maze of swamp.

There is the soft murmur
of people waiting
and dancers preparing
themselves in sacred manner,
as singers hold drums
to licking flames
    and voices
begin the first cycle
of many given our people.

DATE DUE

JUL 1 8 1997	